First World War
and Army of Occupation
War Diary
France, Belgium and Germany

16 DIVISION
48 Infantry Brigade
Royal Munster Fusiliers
9th Battalion
20 December 1915 - 30 May 1916

WO95/1975/5

The Naval & Military Press Ltd
www.nmarchive.com
Published in association with The National Archives

Published by

The Naval & Military Press Ltd

Unit 10 Ridgewood Industrial Park,
Uckfield, East Sussex,
TN22 5QE England
Tel: +44 (0) 1825 749494

www.naval-military-press.com
www.nmarchive.com

This diary has been reprinted in facsimile from the original. Any imperfections are inevitably reproduced and the quality may fall short of modern type and cartographic standards.

© **Crown Copyright**
Images reproduced by permission of The National Archives, London, England, 2015.

Contents

Document type	Place/Title	Date From	Date To
Heading	1975/5 9 Battalion Royal Munster Fusiliers Dec 1915-May 1916		
Heading	16th Division 48th Infy Bde 9th Bn Roy. Munster Fus. Dec 1915-May 1916. Broken U A May 16		
Heading	9th Royal Munster Fusiliers Vol. 1 2d Dec 20.31 Jan 15		
War Diary	Havre	20/12/1915	20/12/1915
War Diary	Noeux Les. Mines	21/12/1915	26/12/1915
War Diary	Nedonchel	27/12/1915	05/01/1916
War Diary	Noeux Les Mines.	06/01/1916	14/01/1916
War Diary	Nedonchel	15/01/1916	26/01/1916
War Diary	Marles Les Mines	27/01/1916	27/01/1916
War Diary	Les Brebis	28/01/1916	31/01/1916
Heading	War. Diary. for 9 (S) Bn Royal Munster Fusrs for month of February 1916		
War Diary	Les Brebis	01/02/1916	01/02/1916
War Diary	S. Maroc	02/02/1916	09/02/1916
War Diary	Les Brebis	10/02/1916	10/02/1916
War Diary	Houchin	11/02/1916	11/02/1916
War Diary	Nedonchel	12/02/1916	14/02/1916
War Diary	Flechin	15/02/1916	27/02/1916
War Diary	Le Cornet Bourdois	28/02/1916	29/02/1916
Heading	9 Batt Roy Muns Fusiles March 1916		
War Diary	Le Cornet Bourdois	01/03/1916	09/03/1916
War Diary	Marles Les Mines	10/03/1916	26/03/1916
War Diary	Trenches Left Sub Section Hulluch	27/03/1916	27/03/1916
War Diary	Trenches	29/03/1916	30/03/1916
War Diary	Philosophe	31/03/1916	31/03/1916
Heading	April 1916		
War Diary	Philosophe	01/04/1916	03/04/1916
War Diary	Trenches	04/04/1916	05/04/1916
War Diary	Left Sub Section Hulluch Section	06/04/1916	06/04/1916
War Diary	Divisional Rest Noeux Les. Mines	07/04/1916	12/04/1916
War Diary	Trenches Bde Support Puis 14 Bis Section.	13/04/1916	15/04/1916
War Diary	Trenches R. Sub. Section Puits 14 Bis Section	16/04/1916	20/04/1916
War Diary	Philosophe East	21/04/1916	24/04/1916
War Diary	Trenches Right Sub Section Puits 14 Bis Section	25/04/1916	29/04/1916
War Diary	Mazingarbe	30/04/1916	30/04/1916
Heading	May 1916		
War Diary	Mazingarbe	01/05/1916	05/05/1916
War Diary	Trenches Left Sub. Section Hulluch Section	06/05/1916	18/05/1916
War Diary	Trenches Right Sub Section Puits 14 Bis Section	19/05/1916	25/05/1916
War Diary	Mazingarbe	26/05/1916	27/05/1916
War Diary	Drouvin.	28/05/1916	30/05/1916

WO 95/5
9 Battalion Royal Munster Fusiliers

Dec 1915 - May 1916

16TH DIVISION
48TH INFY BDE

9TH BN ROY. MUNSTER FUS.
DEC 1915 - MAY 1916.

Broken up May 16

G.H. Royal Tamari Iratinio
18/16
Vol. 1 & 2

Dec 20-31
Jan

16

20 Dec '15 – Jan '16

Army Form C. 2118.

WAR DIARY
or
INTELLIGENCE SUMMARY.
(Erase heading not required.)

Instructions regarding War Diaries and Intelligence Summaries are contained in F. S. Regs., Part II. and the Staff Manual respectively. Title pages will be prepared in manuscript.

Place	Date	Hour	Summary of Events and Information	Remarks and references to Appendices
HAVRE	20/12/15	1am	Disembarked & entrained for NOEUX-LES-MINES.	H.Q.Division Total (comdg. 9th T.M.T
NOEUX-LES-MINES	21/12/15	12 M.N.	Arrived and moved into billets.	
"	22		In billets	
"	23		"	
"	24		"	
"	25		"	
"	26		"	
"	27	8.30 am	Moved into back billets	
"	28		In billets	
"	29		"	
"	30		"	
"	31		"	
"	1/1/16		"	
NEDONCHEL	2/1/16		Battalion in billets. CO & Adjt proceeded to NOEUX-LES-MINES & PHILOSOPHE for attachment to 1st Black Watch. (1st Bde, 1st Divn) for trenches.	
"	3/1/16		Platoons 1, 2, 5 & 6 proceeded to NOEUX-LES-MINES, remainder of Bn in billets at NEDONCHEL.	

WAR DIARY
or
INTELLIGENCE SUMMARY.

Army Form C. 2118.

Place	Date	Hour	Summary of Events and Information	Remarks and references to Appendices
NEDONCHEL	4/1/16		Platoons 1, 2, 5 & 6 proceeded from NOEUX-LES-MINES to PHILOSOPHE for instruction in trenches. Platoons 1 & 2 attached London Scottish, 5 & 6 attached 1st Black Watch (1st Brigade). - Platoons 3, 4, 7 & 8 left NEDONCHEL for NOEUX-LES-MINES. C & D Coys. at NEDONCHEL.	
"	5/1/16		Platoons 3, 4, 7 & 8 joined up with 1, 2, 5 & 6. Whole of A Coy. now with London Scottish, B Coy. with 1st Black Watch. - Battalion H.Q. moved to NOEUX-LES-MINES. C & D Coys at NEDONCHEL.	
NOEUX-LES-MINES.	6/1/16		A & B Coys in trenches, C & D Coys. at NEDONCHEL.	
"	7/1/16		As on 6th.	
"	8/1/16		As on 7th.	
"	9/1/16		A & B Coys in trenches. C & D Coys left NEDONCHEL for NOEUX-LES-MINES.	
"	10/1/16		A & B Coys returned to NOEUX-LES-MINES. Casualties sustained O.R. 2 killed, 9 wounded. - C & D Coys. to PHILOSOPHE for instruction in trenches. D Coy to 1st Camerons (1st Bde, 1st Div.). Attached. C Coy to London Scottish.	
"	11/1/16		A & B Coys at NOEUX-LES-MINES. C & D Coys in trenches.	
"	12/1/16		A & B Coys to back billets NEDONCHEL. C & D Coys still in trenches.	

WAR DIARY
or
INTELLIGENCE SUMMARY

Army Form C. 2118.

Place	Date	Hour	Summary of Events and Information	Remarks and references to Appendices
NOEUX-LES-MINES	13/1/16		C & D Coys returned to NOEUX-LES-MINES from trenches. Casualties sustained O.R. 1 Wounded. A & B Coys at NEDONCHEL.	
"	14/1/16		Bn. HQ & C+D Coys to Back Billets at NEDONCHEL.	
NEDONCHEL	15/1/16		In billets	
"	16/1/16		"	
"	17/1/16		"	
"	18/1/16		"	
"	19/1/16		"	
"	20/1/16		"	
"	21/1/16		"	
"	22/1/16		"	
"	23/1/16		"	
"	24/1/16		"	
"	25/1/16		"	
"	26/1/16		Bn marched to MARLES-LES-MINES.	
MARLES-LES-MINES	27/1/16		MARLES-LES-MINES to LES BREBIS. Attached 141st Inf. Bde. from 2pm 27/1/16 to 9pm 28/1/16. A Coy (Strength 114 O.R. rank) attached as working party to 2/3 London Field Coy R.E. paraded 5.30pm returned to Billets 1.30am 28/1/16.	

Army Form C. 2118.

WAR DIARY
or
INTELLIGENCE SUMMARY.
(Erase heading not required.)

Place	Date	Hour	Summary of Events and Information	Remarks and references to Appendices
LES BREBIS	28/1/16		Bn. provided working parties:- Two Companies with 1/3rd London Field Coy. R.E. in MAROC (B) Section. One Company with 4th " " R.E. " MAROC (A) Section. One Company with 73rd " " R.E. " LOOS Section.	
"	29/1/16		Working parties as on 28/1/16.	
"	30/1/16		" " " " (1 Officer & 40 O.R. attached as Working Party to 11th HANTS in LOOS for 48 hours).	
"	31/1/16		Working parties as on 28/1/16. - Machine Gun Section proceeded 7 p.m. for attachment to 46th Bde. -	

CONFIDENTIAL

WAR DIARY

for

9.(S) Bn Royal Munster Fusrs

for

month of

February 1916

Army Form C. 2118.

WAR DIARY
or
INTELLIGENCE SUMMARY. 9th (Ser) Bn Royal Munster Fusiliers
(Erase heading not required.)

Instructions regarding War Diaries and Intelligence Summaries are contained in F.S. Regs., Part II. and the Staff Manual respectively. Title pages will be prepared in manuscript.

Place	Date	Hour	Summary of Events and Information	Remarks and references to Appendices
LES BREBIS	1.2.16		D Coy. attached to 141st INF BDE in LOOS Sector for 48 hours for instruction in trenches.	
			C " " " 142nd " " " in MAROC " " " " "	
			and attached to 21st LONDON REGT.	
			A & B Coys in Billets in S. MAROC.	H/
S. MAROC	2.2.16		C & D Coys as on 1st	H/
			A & B Coys. working (carrying & digging) parties with 3rd & 4th Field Coys R.E.	
"	3.2.16		A. Coy relieved C. Coy in front line MAROC Sector.	H/
			B " D " " " LOOS "	
			C & D in Billets in S.MAROC.	
"	4.2.16		A & B in front line trenches in MAROC & LOOS Sector respectively	H/
			C & D provided working (carrying & digging) parties for 3rd 4th & 2nd Coy. (LONDON) R.E.	
"	5.2.16		Battalion under orders of Lt. Col. H.B.P. KENNEDY 21st Bn LONDON Regt commanding Right Sub-Section MAROC SECTION. Dispositions as follows:—	H/
			Reference Blue Print Trench map.	
			A Coy. Front line from Boyau 6 Exclusive — Boyau 12 inclusive.	
			B " 1 Platoon (Shregler 1 Officer, 25 O.R.) Garrison ST JAMES KEEP	
			3 Platoons in reserve in Billets in S. MAROC.	
			C " Advanced Support Line from Boyau 3 inclusive — Boyau 11 inclusive	
			D " Front Line Boyau 12 Exclusive to M & C O L [illegible signature] Cmdg. 9th R.M.F.	

Army Form C. 2118.

WAR DIARY
or
INTELLIGENCE SUMMARY.
(Erase heading not required.)   9th (Ser) Bn Royal Munster Fusiliers

Instructions regarding War Diaries and Intelligence Summaries are contained in F.S. Regs., Part II. and the Staff Manual respectively. Title pages will be prepared in manuscript.

Place	Date	Hour	Summary of Events and Information	Remarks and references to Appendices
S. MAROC	6.2.16		Quiet on night - FRENCH. "Left" - 24th Bn LONDON REGT. As on 5th - B Coy. provided digging party for 173rd London Coy. R.E.	M.F.
"	7.2.16		B Coy relieved A Coy in front line. A " to billets in S. MAROC in reserve.	M.F.
"	8.2.16		As on 7th. A & C Coys. provided carrying parties for (173rd M.) LONDON Coys. R.E.	M.F.
"	9.2.16		Battalion relieved by 17th Bn LONDON REGT & marched to billets in LES BREBIS. Casualties during period 1st - 9th February O.R. 9 wounded.	M.F.
LES BREBIS	10.2.16		Battalion marched from LES BREBIS to billets at HOUCHIN.	M.F.
HOUCHIN	11.2.16		" " HOUCHIN to back billets at NEDONCHEL.	M.F.
NEDONCHEL	12.2.16		In billets. Lt Colonel E. MONTEAGLE-BROWNE assumed command of the Battalion vice Lt Colonel H.F. WILLIAMS.	M.F.
"	13.2.16		Battalion attended Divine Service Parade at 9 a.m. - Bathing at 16th DIVISIONAL BATHS at FLECHINELLE. Clean underclothing provided.	M.F.
"	14.2.16		Battalion marched to new billeting area at FLECHIN (Sheet 36 M.A. Square S.14), moving off at 10 a.m. and arriving in FLECHIN at 12 noon. - Billets very	M.F.

Lt Col E Monteagle Browne
Comdg 9th R M F

Army Form C. 2118.

WAR DIARY
or
INTELLIGENCE SUMMARY.
(Erase heading not required.)

9th (Sev) Bn Royal Munster Fusiliers

Instructions regarding War Diaries and Intelligence Summaries are contained in F.S. Regs., Part II. and the Staff Manual respectively. Title pages will be prepared in manuscript.

Place	Date	Hour	Summary of Events and Information	Remarks and references to Appendices
FLECHIN	14/2/16	-	Compact, clean and comfortable, and the whole Battalion were billeted in the Town. Band with pipers played at each every evening, much enjoyed by the troops. A long valley NW of the village provided a most excellent place for musketry & machine gun practice. Special targets were made by the Battalion Pioneers and 2 Practices were commenced.	
"	15/2/16	-	Battalion continued training in Billets with musketry. Bombing ground was laid out and practice started with dummy and live Grenades under supervision of Lieut. Fitz-Gerald. Snipers under 2/Lt Lyne. Sanitary arrangements of Battalion showed considerable improvement under Regimental Medical officer Captain R.R. WETTENHALL. R.A.M.C. and specially commended.	
"	16/2/16		Continuance of training in Billets. Musketry. Bombing, etc. Special attention paid to Physical training with rifles to strengthen arms for Bayonet fighting. Saluting with & without arms. Bayonet fighting under instruction of Lt. FURNEY, also received special attention.	
"	17/2/16		Battalion was inspected by Major-General W.B. HICKIE, C.B. Commanding 16th (IRISH) Division accompanied by Brig.-General F.W. RAMSAY, D.S.O. Commanding	

F. Montagu Bradish O'Neill

Army Form C. 2118.

WAR DIARY
or
INTELLIGENCE SUMMARY.
(Erase heading not required.) 9. (Ser) B⁾ Royal MUNSTER Fusiliers

Place	Date	Hour	Summary of Events and Information	Remarks and references to Appendices
FLECHIN	18/2/16		48th Infantry Brigade, when the Officers and men were highly praised on the improvement shewn and small turnout. Battalion transport was specially commended for its excellent appearance. Major-General Hickie to Reserve Commander —	
"	19/2/16		Continuance of training in Billets. (Musketry, Bombing, Drill, etc.). Inspection of Battalion by Commanding Officer after special fitting of equipment and packing of valise. Belts waterproof sheet under flap of valise, and mackintosh cape rolled on top of valise — Address by G.O.C. 48th INFANTRY BRIGADE, complimentary remarks —	
"	20/2/16		Continuance of training in Billets. The shooting carried out at Home in very bad weather no higher criterion of shooting abilities of the Battalion. ∴ Good shots were allowed 6 rounds fires to fillets and 3rd class shots repeated several times. Practices with pronounced success.	
"	21/2/16		Inspection of Battalion by Lt. General Sir HUBERT GOUGH, G.O.C. 1st Corps. Battalion drawn up on Square FLECHIN- Machine Gun detachment MontyghBrae Jh Ethel C.N.9th R.M.F.	

Army Form C. 2118.

WAR DIARY
or
INTELLIGENCE SUMMARY.

(Erase heading not required.) 9*(Sv) Bⁿ Royal Mounted Fusiliers

Summary of Events and Information in LOOS benched

Place	Date	Hour	Summary of Events and Information	Remarks and references to Appendices
FLECHIN	22/2/16		on return from attachment to 15th DIVISION, paraded with Battalion. The turn out of all ranks was very specially commended by the CORPS Commander, who was also pleased with Company Cookers and cooking arrangements, and the Transport seen.	
"	23/2/16		Training in Billets continued. Very useful instruction of putting men through trenches wearing Gas Helmets being carried out. It was necessary for the men to clean the Eye pieces inside of condensed moisture by rubbing on forehead. Shooting was very good considering the handicaps.	
"	24/2/16		Musketry, Bombing, & general training of Battalion continued. Mincing Machines ("per Company") were taken into use. Scraps of meat, bacon, biscuits etc. being ground up and made into rissoles making a nice change for the men. Battalion drawn up in the Square, FLECHIN, for inspection by Sir CHARLES MUNRO, G.O.C. 1st Army. Heavy snow continually fell for the past 16 hours and eventually caused a postponement	

F.Mortagh Brezle Cht
Cdg 9Sv B. 9th

Army Form C. 2118.

WAR DIARY
or
INTELLIGENCE SUMMARY.
(Erase heading not required.)   9- (Sev) B: Royal Munster Fusiliers

Place	Date	Hour	Summary of Events and Information	Remarks and references to Appendices
FLECHIN	25/2/16		of the inspection.	
	26/2/16		Continuance of General Training of Battalion - Musketry, Bombing, Signalling, Snipers, Machine Gunners. Inspection of Billets, Rifles, Ammunition, Equipment & Kit by Commanding Officer & Workshops - Pioneers, Tailors & Shoemakers especially good in the Regiment. The two first named quickly producing articles necessary for having & the two last named a source of comfort to the men and a saving of money to the public. - 25 pairs of boots & repaired daily by Sergeant Shoemaker and 4 Assistants.	
	27/2/16		Battalion marched to new Billeting Area at LE CORNET BOURDOIS (Sheet 36 A O 28.34.35) moving off at 9 a.m. - Route via LIGNY-LEZ-AIRE, COTTES, LILLERS) and arriving at LE CORNET BOURDOIS at 1.30 p.m. Billets scattered. Barns roomy, clean and comfortable for men. Country flat and nearly all arable, consequently difficult for training, only roadways and small orchards available.	

H Wintergale Bonner Sr C Steel
Cmdg 9th R.M.F.

Army Form C. 2118.

WAR DIARY
or
INTELLIGENCE SUMMARY.
(Erase heading not required.)

9th (Sv) Bn Royal Munster Fusiliers

Instructions regarding War Diaries and Intelligence Summaries are contained in F.S. Regs., Part II. and the Staff Manual respectively. Title pages will be prepared in manuscript.

Place	Date	Hour	Summary of Events and Information	Remarks and references to Appendices
LE CORNET BOURDOIS	28/1/16		Battalion at nine hours notice in G.H.Q. reserve. Reconnaissances made of routes to entraining station. Training carried on. Musketry - only available ranges for musketry and machine gun firing on those flat areas are Railway Embankment. Physical Training - special attention paid to strengthening of arms for Bayonet fighting - Instruction of Companies in execution in Grenadier work under 2nd Lt BAILY. Battalion Grenadier Officer. SICK. just under 3% of Battalion sick - chiefly colds & rheumatism. Practice in Bayonet fighting & Company Drill. - Special musketry instruction to 3rd class shots under Lt MAHONY (Battalion musketry officer) - Short Route march.	TK TK TK TK TK
"	29/1/16		Following Courses were attended by Officers rOR of the Battalion during the month:- 16th Divisional Grenade School. 1 Officer 10 O.R.	

Montgomery Brown Lt Colonel
Cmdg 9 R.M.F.

Army Form C. 2118.

WAR DIARY
or
INTELLIGENCE SUMMARY.
(Erase heading not required.)

9'B" Royal Munster Fus'rs

Place	Date	Hour	Summary of Events and Information	Remarks and references to Appendices
			16" Divisional Wiring Class 2 Officers, 32 O.R.	
			1st Army Anti-Gas School + 5 O.R.	
			G. 16" Division Engineering Class 1 Officer	
			16" Division Pioneer Class — 8 O.R.	
			16" Division Trench Mortar Class 1 Officer 1 O.R.	
			F.W.M.Inglis Major in Chd.	
			Cmdg. 9th R.M.F.	

9 Bett Road Hugh Fussell

Dr Fussell — March 1916

Army Form C. 2118.

WAR DIARY
or
INTELLIGENCE SUMMARY.

9ᵗʰ (Sev) 13ᵗʰ Royal Munster Fusiliers

(Erase heading not required.)

Place	Date	Hour	Summary of Events and Information	Remarks and references to Appendices
LE CORNET BOURDOIS	1/3/16	—	Training carried on:- Close Order drill, Manual of Arms, saluting, Extended order drill, Field practice of assault. Combination route march. — Companies proceeding independently to a given point to arrive at stated times. Three companies arrived on time, one Company 8 minutes late. Signallers practised in getting into touch with Companies on the move. — Following promotions appeared in "Gazette" of 28ᵗʰ February and "London Gazette" of 28ᵗʰ February :- Lieutenants to be Captains: R.A. FRIZELL, J.P. HARDING, J.C. WATTS-RUSSELL, F.E. FURNEY, M.H. FITZGERALD, J.R. COLFER. 2ⁿᵈ Lieuts to be Lieutenants. Promotions to date from December 14ᵗʰ 1915. 5 N.C.O.'s returned from course at 1ˢᵗ Army Cook-gas school. AIRE, and were detailed to lecture to Companies on knowledge gained. Lieut FURNEY, Instructor, Battalion	
"	2/3/16		Officers class for Bayonet fighting instruction under Lieut FURNEY, Battalion Physical drill & Bayonet fighting Specialist started — 7.15 - 8 a.m. daily Training:- Tactical Grenade work, Bayonet fighting, Close order drill, manual of Arms. — Lectures on "Nature of Explosives, Grenades 1, 3 & 5	

J. Montagu Browne Lᵗ. Col.
Comdg: 9ᵗʰ (6) Bn. Royal Munster Fusiliers

Army Form C. 2118.

WAR DIARY
or
INTELLIGENCE SUMMARY.

(Erase heading not required.) 9 (S) B. Royal Munster Fusiliers

Instructions regarding War Diaries and Intelligence Summaries are contained in F. S. Regs., Part II. and the Staff Manual respectively. Title pages will be prepared in manuscript.

Place	Date	Hour	Summary of Events and Information	Remarks and references to Appendices
			"The Meeting of Gas Attacks" "Machine Gun in Trench Warfare" were delivered by Company Commanders and Machine Gun Officer (Lt MORAN). 8 Sergeants returned from attachment to 1st Bn for instruction in Trench Warfare. MK	
LE CORNET BOURDOIS	3/3/16		Heavy rain & snow fell in the morning and continued till midday. Nearly all training grounds under water and generally in bad state, performed Battalion engaged in cleaning of equipment, ammunition, clothing in Billets.— Conference of Commanding Officers at 48th Infantry Brigade Headquarters at 3.45 p.m. Major General W B HICKIE Commanding 16th Irish Division lectured to Officers of 48th Brigade at School, HAM EN ARTOIS on Trench Warfare. 16 Officers from Battalion attended.— Attention drawn in Battalion Orders that men must not move outside limits of Battalion Billeting area.— MK	

F Montgomery Lt Colonel
Comdg: 9th (S) Bn. Royal Munster Fusiliers

Army Form C. 2118.

WAR DIARY
or
INTELLIGENCE SUMMARY.
(Erase heading not required.)

9th (Ser) Bn Royal Munster Fusiliers

Instructions regarding War Diaries and Intelligence Summaries are contained in F.S. Regs., Part II and the Staff Manual respectively. Title pages will be prepared in manuscript.

Place	Date	Hour	Summary of Events and Information	Remarks and references to Appendices
LE CORNET BOURDOIS	4/3/16	—	Morning very wet, rain + snow fell heavily, necessitating having being carried on in billets. - Manual of Arms, Saluting drill, Inspections of Equipment and kits by Company Commanders. A.D.M.S. 16th DIVISION medically inspected 30 men paraded as medically and otherwise unfit for duties in the trenches.	
	5/3/16	—	Sunday. - Roman Catholics attended Divine Service at 9.30 a.m. - Church of England at 4 p.m. - Battalion paraded at 11 a.m. for presentation of Parchment Certificate to Lt. FURNEY, by G.O.C. 48th Infantry Brigade. THE IRISH BRIGADE "I have read with much pleasure the report of your Regimental Commander and Brigade Commander regarding your gallant conduct and devotion to duty in the field on Feb. 1916, and have ordered your name and deed to be entered in the record of the Irish Division. (Signed) W.B. HICKIE Major-General Commanding 16th IRISH DIVISION	

EMontagehBride
Lt: Colonel,
Comdg: 9th (S) Bn. Royal Munster Fusiliers.

WAR DIARY
or
INTELLIGENCE SUMMARY.

9th (Ser) Bn Royal Munster Fusiliers

Army Form C. 2118.

Place	Date	Hour	Summary of Events and Information	Remarks and references to Appendices
LE CORNET BOURDOIS	5/3/16		Previous to presentation G.O.C. 48th Brigade inspected the Battalion & expressed his satisfaction at the continued improvement in steadiness, bearing and steadiness on parade of the men and subsequently witnessed march past in column of route. — Two field Guns belonging to 1st field Gun and how to subsequently concealed Batteries by Companies were given practical demonstration by Artillery officers of mounting of 18 p/r field Gun, manner of putting out of action, and working of sights. Officers showed much interest and appeared anxious to learn all about the guns which was on view for 2 hours. 2/Lieut Casey Battalion Bomb-Shot Officer & 8 men returned from Course of Instruction at 16th DIVISIONAL Grenade School, LAIRES. 1/	
"	6/3/16		D Company found following working parties for 138th Coy. R.E. 80 men for work on flying ground, HESDIGNEUL	

HMontgomery
Lt: Colonel,
Comdg: 9th (S) Bn. Royal Munster Fusiliers.

WAR DIARY or INTELLIGENCE SUMMARY

Army Form C. 2118.

9th Bn: Royal Munster Fusiliers

Place: FOSSE BRUAY.

40 men for work on FOSSE BRUAY. Parties proceeded by Motor Lorries at 7.30 a.m. returning at 4.30 p.m. —
Training carried on:- Physical training 7 – 7.30 a.m.
Lt: Bally, Battalion Grenadier Officer instructed A,B,& C. Companies in succession in Grenadier work.— Wiring parties under 2/Lt Cary.— Manual of arms, Extended order drill etc.—
Medical Officer Captain Wetenhall lectured on Sanitation in and about Billets".—
2nd class shots were exercised in Trigger pressing, rapid loading, by 2/Lt graham, Battalion Musketry Officer."—
Lt:Colonel E. MONTEAGLE-BROWNE lectured 6 Officers of 48th Infantry Brigade at HAM-EN-ARTOIS on "Co-operation of Artillery with Infantry in the field". Brig-General E.J.DUFFUS, C.B. Commanding 16th Divisional Artillery was in the chair. Several Artillery Officers and 15 Officers from each Battalion in the 48th Brigade were present.

Monteagle Browne
Lt: Colonel,
Comdg: 9th (S) Bn. Royal Munster Fusiliers.

Army Form C. 2118.

WAR DIARY
or
INTELLIGENCE SUMMARY.
(Erase heading not required.) 9 (S) Bn Royal Munster Fusiliers

Instructions regarding War Diaries and Intelligence Summaries are contained in F. S. Regs., Part II. and the Staff Manual respectively. Title pages will be prepared in manuscript.

Place	Date	Hour	Summary of Events and Information	Remarks and references to Appendices
LE CORNET BOURDOIS	7/3/16		Training carried on: Bombing, Wiring, Bayonet fighting, Manual of Arms.— Afternoon: Route march.— Veterinary Officer attached to 118th Infantry Brigade lectured to all mounted Officers and personnel of transport on Care and management of horses and mules.	
"	8/3/16		Training continued in Wiring, Bayonet fighting, Manual of Arms etc. Battalion Snipers under 2/Lt LYNE, Sniping Officer specially instructed in use of Telescopic Sights and Sniperscopes. Company Commanders lectured on March Discipline, dress & bearing, and saluting, when off tour.— Commanding Officer lectured at 6 p.m. to all Officers and N.C.O's of the Battalion on Discipline affecting Leave, dangers of venereal diseases, Duties in trenches.— Two Officers and 20 O.R. attended demonstration of FLAMMENWERFER.	

McInleyBrode
Lt Colonel,
Comdg: 9th (S) Bn. Royal Munster Fusiliers.

Army Form C. 2118.

WAR DIARY
or
INTELLIGENCE SUMMARY.

(Erase heading not required.) 9 (S) Bn. Royal Munster Fusiliers

Place	Date	Hour	Summary of Events and Information	Remarks and references to Appendices
LE CORNET BOURDOIS	9/3/16		The Battalion moved into the 1st Corps Reserve Area and proceeded by march route to Billets at MARLES LES MINES. Marched off at 10 a.m. Route via LILLERS & LOZINGHEM, arriving in MARLES-LES-MINES at 12.40 p.m. Billets roomy, clean & comfortable. 3 Companies billeted in Corons, 1 in Barns. Good natural granies afforded excellent rifle ranges up to 50 yards for machine Gun Section and Companies firing. Trenches for practice in Grenade throwing were found to be dug by Units previously billeted here. Bells aeroplanes dropped bombs on railway line in vicinity of Lillers, but no casualties reported. GOC 1st Army was to have inspected the Brigade on line of march, in his absence GOC 16th Division & GOC 48th Infantry Brigade accompanied witnessed the march through LILLERS, and expressed great satisfaction at the smartness of the men and steady bearing.	

E. M. Stephens
Lt. Colonel,
Comdg: 9th (S) Bn. Royal Munster Fusiliers.

Army Form C. 2118.

WAR DIARY
or
INTELLIGENCE SUMMARY.

(Erase heading not required.) 9- (Sv) B.: Royal Munster Fusiliers

Instructions regarding War Diaries and Intelligence Summaries are contained in F. S. Regs., Part II. and the Staff Manual respectively. Title pages will be prepared in manuscript.

Place	Date	Hour	Summary of Events and Information	Remarks and references to Appendices
MARLES LES MINES	10/3/16		Training carried on: Musketry on Range.— Bayonet fighting, saluting and Close Order Drill & Manual of Arms.— Afternoon — Route March.— D Company Bombers classified by Battalion Grenadier Officer, who reported throwing very good.— Sketches Scheme under instruction of Medical Officer.— W	
"	11/3/16		Very fine Spring day. Training continued under most favourable weather conditions. Firing by Companies and Machine Gun section on 30 yards range. Results good.— Smoke Helmet Drill, training instruction, training of Scouts.— W	
"	12/3/16		Sunday.— Divine Service parades Roman Catholics 9am.— Church of England 11 am.— W Father FOSSE & 3 Archer were attached to battalion from Brigade	

G.W. Naughton?
Lt. Colonel,
Comdg: 9th (S) Bn. Royal Munster Fusiliers.

WAR DIARY or INTELLIGENCE SUMMARY

9th (S) Bn. Royal Munster Fusiliers

Army Form C. 2118.

Place	Date	Hour	Summary of Events and Information	Remarks and references to Appendices
MARLES LES MINES	13/3/16		Very fine day. Baths at No 3 FOSSE AUCHEL were allotted to the Battalion from 8 am - 12 noon - 240 men per hour can be bathed there by good management - New underclothing was issued. - B Coy continued firing on 30 yds range on return from baths - Other Companies exercised in Wiring, Grenade throwing, Drill & manual of Arms. - Lieut. E.F. COLLINS reported arrival for duty with the Battalion. This officer was previously with the Regiment, but transferred to Royal Flying Corps.	
	14/3/16		Lieut-General Sir Hubert Gough, Commanding 1st Corps visited the Battalion and saw Companies at training - machine gun detachment firing on range. D Coy firing and Wiring Class. Afternoon was devoted to ROUTE MARCH to AUCHEL Ferdinand and baths were for half an hour. Battalion addressed by Commanding Officer on discipline.	

Elliot-Lockhart-Bruce
Colonel,
Comdg: 9th (S) Bn. Royal Munster Fusiliers.

Army Form C. 2118.

WAR DIARY
or
INTELLIGENCE SUMMARY.

(Erase heading not required.) 9 (Sv) Bn Royal Munster Fusiliers

Place	Date	Hour	Summary of Events and Information	Remarks and references to Appendices
MARLES LES MINES.	15/3/16		Training – Physical training, Bayonet fighting, Short Helmet drill, etc. – C Coy Musketry on range.– Commanding Officer, Adjutant, Intelligence Officer and Company Commanders proceeded by motor bus to VERMELLES and reconnoitred left sub-sector of HULLUCH Sector to be taken over by Battalion. — H	
"	16/3/16		Training carried on. Working party 2 Officers, 5 NCOs & 100 men provided to work on AUCHEL Aerodrome.– 6 NCOs of Battalion inspected by Commanding Officer and passed out Successfully as qualified Instructors in Bayonet fighting. Notification that Corps Commander would inspect Brigade on 17th inst. H	

H Montagu Bates
Lt. Colonel
Comdg: 9th S Royal Munster Fusiliers.

Army Form C. 2118.

WAR DIARY
or
INTELLIGENCE SUMMARY.
(Erase heading not required.)   9 (S) Bn Royal Munster Fusiliers

Place	Date	Hour	Summary of Events and Information	Remarks and references to Appendices
MARLES LES MINES	17/3/16		ST PATRICK'S DAY. Divine Service Parades – Roman Catholics 8·45 am. Church of England 9 am. Corps Commander's inspection of 48th Brigade postponed. Brigade Sports in afternoon – General Sir Charles Monro C.B. Commanding First Army present. Battalion tied in following events. Grenadiers individual & battalion, Machine Gun competition, Tug-of-War, Dancing and Mule race, and second in Boxing competition. – W Draft of 13 men arrived. I recently sent to Base as medically unfit by A.D.M.S. 16th Division, included in reinforcement. – W	
	18/3/16		Morning – Short route march. Afternoon – Battalion Hockey Team played A.S.C. – W	

F Montagu Burdon
Lt. Colonel,
Comdg: 9th (S) Bn Royal Munster Fusiliers.

Army Form C. 2118.

WAR DIARY
or
INTELLIGENCE SUMMARY.
(Erase heading not required.)

9th (Sv) Bn Royal Munster Fusiliers

Instructions regarding War Diaries and Intelligence Summaries are contained in F. S. Regs., Part II. and the Staff Manual respectively. Title pages will be prepared in manuscript.

Place	Date	Hour	Summary of Events and Information	Remarks and references to Appendices
MARLES LES MINES	19/3/16		Divine Service parade - Roman Catholics in LOZINGHEM church 9am. Band attended - Church of England 10.30 am. Visiting parties operation 1 NCO & 50 OR. for work on BETHUNE RANGE. Motor Lorries conveyed party. 2 Officers, 5 NCOs & 100 OR. for work at AUCHEL aerodrome. Lt Col BISHOP (very good) & 9 OR. qualified as Stokes Gunners at course of Stokes Trench Mortars held at BOURECQ from 5.3.16 - 11.3.16.- W	
"	20/3/16		Training - A Coy. Musketry on range. - Other Companies - Physical training. Bayonet fighting. Close & extended order drill. Smoke helmet drill. Knots of arms - thing- Commanding Officer lectured to all Officers and NCOs. on "keeping order on sentry", "taking over of, and duties in trenches - W.	

EWorthington
Lt Colonel
Comdg: 9th (S) Bn Royal Munster Fusiliers

Army Form C. 2118.

WAR DIARY
or
INTELLIGENCE SUMMARY.

(Erase heading not required.)

9th Bn Royal Munster Fusiliers

Instructions regarding War Diaries and Intelligence Summaries are contained in F. S. Regs., Part II. and the Staff Manual respectively. Title pages will be prepared in manuscript.

Place	Date	Hour	Summary of Events and Information	Remarks and references to Appendices
MARLES LES MINES	21/3/16		Training carried on. Musketry, Bombing, Bayonet fighting, Drill, etc. G.O.C. 1st Bde (Sir Hubert Gough) visited Companies at work, accompanied by G.O.C. 48th Infantry Brigade & Commanding Officer. 15 Officers & N.C.O.s attended lecture & demonstration in Rifle Grenades at 16th Divisional Grenade School, LABEUVRIERE. C. of C. Or. Tossit list and Beer (Free) ord. by Commanding Officer as gratified instructors in Bayonet fighting. J.B.	
"	22/3/16		Training as on 31st. Battalion bathed at FOSSE No 3 AUCHEL. — Steam undressing ranced. G.O.C 48th Bde present. Battalion turned very inadequate. J.B.	
"	23/3/16		Training in Romp, Bombing, Bayonet fighting, Musketry. Lunch in hra Officers & O.R., Lunch hr an Officers & O.R., saying officers Machine Gun Officer & O.R., Lunch hr an Officer & O.R. saying officers of A O.R & H B Coy allow proceeded to learn geography of LEFT SUB-	

J Montagh Bates Lt. Colonel
Comdg. 9th Bn R. Munster Fusiliers

WAR DIARY
or
INTELLIGENCE SUMMARY.

Army Form C. 2118.

9 (S) B. Royal Munster Fusiliers

Place	Date	Hour	Summary of Events and Information	Remarks and references to Appendices
MARLES LES MINES	2/3/16		SECTION, HULLUCH SECTOR, prior to the taking over of the line by Battalion. Details attached to 12 B. H.L.I. further 5 Offs & O.R. attended Gas and demonstration in Rifle Grenades at 16. Divisional School, LABEUVRIERE. Training in special subject carried on. Machine Gun, Bombing, wiring &c. (attend 2nd Lt. N. BOSTON attached to Bn from 7. ROYAL IRISH FUS.	
	3/3/16		2nd in command & Company Offrs & Grenadier Officer, 1 Officer + 32 O.R. of Machine Gun Section to C.O. 7 y. Battery Ry. Signallers proceeded to photo torn trenches from HULLERS thence by motor work to LEFT SUB SECTION, HULLUCH SECTOR to reconnoitre trenches to be occupied by unit. Battalion engaged in preparations for evacuation of billets, collection of Stores, checking of equipment, etc. Combined bands of 9 Munsters & O. R. Dublin played as usual.	

J Monteagle Browne Lt. Colonel
Commdg 9th (S) Bn Royal Munster Fusiliers

Army Form C. 2118.

WAR DIARY
or
INTELLIGENCE SUMMARY.
(Erase heading not required) 9 (S) B. Royal Munster Fusiliers

Place	Date	Hour	Summary of Events and Information	Remarks and references to Appendices
MARLES LES MINES	26/ 9/15		Dismounted portion of Battalion moved off at 7.40 a.m. to LAPUGNOY Station, entraining for NOEUX-LES-MINES. Arrived there 9.15 a.m. and proceeded by march route to take over LEFT SUB-SECTION, HULLUCH SECTOR. Long wait from 10.35 a.m. – 2.30 p.m. at MAZINGARBE, where got dinner. Men much footsore from travelling. Field Kitchens pushed forward by road. Via PLACE À BRUAY & NOEUX LES MINES. Guides from 13th H.L.I. were met at VERMELLES – PHILOSOPHE X ROADS at 2.30 p.m. Relief complete 6.15 p.m. Dispositions 3 Companies in front line, one in Support, one in Reserve trenches. Frontage occupied 800 yards – from STONE STREET to HAY ALLEY. No casualties sustained during relief.	
			At 6.31 p.m. Enemy Exploded 2 mines causing large craters at H.13.a. 15.20 and H.13.c.4.9. Destroying about 70 yds of fire trench. Twelve Dublin Fusiliers killed. ESSEX LANE, HAY ALLEY, Support and Reserve trenches &c were simultaneously active with rifle grenades and trench mortars. The 13th Grenadiers occupied near and far lips of craters, notwithstanding the attempts of the enemy to occupy the edge of the craters with bombing parties. –	

F.W. Whitaker B.A. Lt. Colonel

Army Form C. 2118.

WAR DIARY
or
INTELLIGENCE SUMMARY.
(Erase heading not required.) 9 (S) B: Royal Munster Fusiliers

Instructions regarding War Diaries and Intelligence Summaries are contained in F.S. Regs., Part II. and the Staff Manual respectively. Title pages will be prepared in manuscript.

Place	Date	Hour	Summary of Events and Information	Remarks and references to Appendices
TRENCHES LEFT-SUB-SECTION HULLUCH	27/3/16		Enemy were driven back by machine gun and rifle fire. A number of N.C.O.s and men were buried by the debris, but most of them were dug-out & killed or ?unaccounted for. Activity with rifle grenades and machine gun & rifle fire continued throughout the night. 2/Lt BAILY, Grenadier Officer, and Capt SH/EDRICS & 2/Lt CASEY showed special promptitude in dealing with the situation effectively. Continuous activity throughout the day & night on the enemy's side with French mortars and Rifle Grenades, the latter being particularly troublesome. Front line extended on right to HOLLY ROW ??????? 3 Companies in front line, 1 in support. 1 Company of 9: DUBLINS Relieving Portion of the trench which was destroyed by Subsidence of reserve. - Portion of trenches caused in with difficulty owing to movement on 26:th commenced. Work was resumed with difficulty owing to NORTHERN double machine gun and rifle fire. - Saps running out to NORTHERN craters were started. - Officers Patrol scanned Enemy's wire all along our front. This reported to be in good repair, with Chevaux de Frise & late wire Entg Enemy killed on night of 26/27, seen lying close up to Enemy parapet B	

J.H.W.Nigh.O'Brady

Army Form C. 2118.

WAR DIARY
or
INTELLIGENCE SUMMARY.
(Erase heading not required.)

9-(S) B? Royal Munster Fusiliers

Place	Date	Hour	Summary of Events and Information	Remarks and references to Appendices
TRENCHES	29/3/16		Enemy continuously active over whole of front & support lines with Rifle Grenades and Trench Mortars. — Having of Enemy mine having reached 30 yards of our parapet, necessitated left Garrison of the left of right company modifying fire intermittently during the night.	
"	30/3/16		Enemy Mine exploded at H.13 c.4.5.7½ at 8.45 am and simultaneously bombarded with French Mortars & rifle Grenades. — No craters visible. — 400 rifle Grenades were fired by us, with effective results. — Officers Patrol went out to investigate reports flying near CORDIFF SAP. Patrol missed did not argue that Enemy emerged from Enemy mining. — Battalion relieved by 7th/8th Royal Irish Rifles, and proceeded to Brigade Reserve at PHILOSOPHE. Casualties during 4 days tour of trenches:- 7 O.R. Killed. 22 O.R. wounded. 17 O.R. missing, believed killed. — Trench strength 373. — Owing to abnormal activity of Enemy and consequent loss of rest, all ranks very fatigued and in much need of sleep. All Company remain in Reserve line trench. —	

H.Montagh Bird
Lt. Colonel
Comdg 9th Bt. Royal Munster Fusiliers

Army Form C. 2118.

WAR DIARY
or
INTELLIGENCE SUMMARY.

(Erase heading not required.) 9th (S) Bn Royal Munster Fusiliers

Place	Date	Hour	Summary of Events and Information	Remarks and references to Appendices
PHILO-SOPHE	31/3/16		Bn in Brigade Reserve at 1/2 hours notice. — Working parties for french maintenance provided — also carrying parties. — Baths at 2nd INCN R.E. and clean underclothing provided — BC	

JWMonteagleBrowne
Lt Colonel

April 1416

Army Form C. 2118 **4**

XVI

WAR DIARY
or
INTELLIGENCE SUMMARY.

(Erase heading not required.)

9-(S) B: Royal Munster Fusiliers

Instructions regarding War Diaries and Intelligence Summaries are contained in F.S. Regs., Part II. and the Staff Manual respectively. Title pages will be prepared in manuscript.

Place	Date	Hour	Summary of Events and Information	Remarks and references to Appendices
PHILOSOPHE	1/4/16	—	(less 1 Coy.) Battalion in Billets in Brigade Reserve.— Carrying parties for R.E. provided, and working party of 1 Off. & 50 O.R. for Trench Maintenance.— Work on WINGSWAY.— repair of trench boards, clearing of mud in trenches, sump holes cleared.— MK	
"	2/4/16	—	Battalion, less 1 Coy. in Brigade Reserve.— Carrying parties for R.E. and Trench Maintenance working party provided.— MK	
"	3/4/16	—	Battalion relieved 7" B: Royal Irish Rifles in LEFT SUB-SECTION, HULLUCH SECTION.— Relief commenced at 3.30 p.m. and all Coys reported complete at 6.15 p.m. Disposition. 3 Companies in Front line, 1 in Support left.— 1 Company of 7" B: Royal Irish Rifles and 3 Platoons of 9" B: Royal Dublin Fusiliers in Reserve Trench and at disposal of O.O. LEFT SUB-SECTION for working and carrying parties.—	

F Montephonse Lt. Colonel,
Comdg: 9th (S) Bn. Royal Munster Fusiliers.

Army Form C. 2118.

WAR DIARY
or
INTELLIGENCE SUMMARY.

(Erase heading not required.) 9-(S) B= Royal Munster Fusiliers

Place	Date	Hour	Summary of Events and Information	Remarks and references to Appendices
	3/4/16	—	Relief completed without casualties —	
TRENCHES	4/4/16	—	Enemy displayed considerable activity with Rifle Grenades, Trench Mortars and Aerial Torpedoes throughout night 3/4th April and during the day of 4th. Bomb proof shelters were erected along front lines. — Debris thrown up by Enemy mine Explosions on night of 26th March was considerably cleared, and communication re-established in front line between HAY ALLEY and SOUTHERN SAP which was closed up by Enemy K mine Explosions — the shifts were lengthened in the damaged portions of the trench and instead of what before in an effective fighting state the enemy was in good condition but that no addition has been made to the present front line. Mortars obtained few direct hits on the enemy front line during the day. We are not otherwise with 5 grenades. Sounds of enemy mining were detected at various points of our front. The O.C. Tunnelling Coy. 3/175. M.B. has begun countermining in our sector.	
	5/4/16	—	Front line from SOUTHERN SAP to HAY ALLEY was deepened and the sapped on our part of the line. The listener was reopened and repaired. FLY LANE was thoroughly opened up. We found a good communication tunnel which could be opened to Caldwin as a protection for the Left flank of the Section. 35 ft of new were erected. Tapping was heard in the vicinity of G16.1. Signalling by lamp was obtained in the German lines opposite H13.2. between 10 & 11 pm. The enemy Sap which had been started E of NORTHERN CRATER was yesterday finished by	Lt: Colonel Comdg: 9th (S) Bn. Royal Munster Fusiliers

Army Form C. 2118.

WAR DIARY
or
INTELLIGENCE SUMMARY.

(Erase heading not required.) 9 (S) Bn: Royal Munster Fusiliers

Place	Date	Hour	Summary of Events and Information	Remarks and references to Appendices
TRENCHES LEFT SUB-SECTION HULLUCH	5/4/16		The Battalion Bombers set to work on the work abandoned the previous day by a detachment with all grenades and several torpedoes along our front. The Sapping was however organised & a fortnum's dump of gelignite bombs, bombs, brown's dump from HOLLY LANE to TRALEE CRATER with branch northern and left flanks. Cover for proposed saps etc also dug etc & movements apparent and new work was seen to flag into the air.	✓
HULLUCH SECTION	6/4/16		The parapet of the post had been blown HOLLY LANE to STONE STREET was shelled and made bullet proof. The Battalion was relieved by the 6TH MUNSTERS and proceeded to Divisional Rest at NOEUX LES MINES. The Shrub Bath men were excellent. The Brenades had been considerably improved (on? symphatum and fuzes were butcher more in a clean and tidy condition owing to fuse greater care in storage munitions). Casualties First Circuit arising (from 3/4/16 - 5/4/16): Wounded (at duty) 2civs.2. W.T. the Vergt. Killed: 1 O.R. Wounded: 14 O.R.	✓
DIVISION AL REST - NOEUX-LES MINES	7/4/16		The Battalion were employed in cleaning their huts and kit. Inspections of arms and equipment were held by Major & flushing Officers etc. A Reinforcement Draft of 57 O.R. arrived and was posted to a Coy. The Band played at attend at 6 p.m.	✓
	8/4/16		A guard for Divisional Headquarters at NOEUX LES MINES of 1 NCO & 3 men was found by the Battalion. The Battalion found fatigue Working parties to R.E. at NOEUX and at BETHUNE. Lieut Osborne & 4 O.R. proceeded on leave.	✓
	9/4/16		Divine Service Parade, R.C. in NOEUX LES MINES church at 9 am, C of E. in YMCA Hut at 11.30 am. The Battalion paraded at 11.30 am in Smith road Marched to VERQUIN about 2 m in heavy rain. After luncheon was Field Gun Col. 9th Division Percival Field. Then Reached in the Rattalion	✓

F. W. Fitzgerald Brooke Lt: Col 7/4/16
Comdg: 9th (S) Bn. Royal Munster Fusiliers

Army Form C. 2118.

WAR DIARY
or
INTELLIGENCE SUMMARY

(Erase heading not required.) 7 (S) Bn. Royal Munster Fusiliers

Instructions regarding War Diaries and Intelligence Summaries are contained in F.S. Regs., Part II. and the Staff Manual respectively. Title pages will be prepared in manuscript.

Place	Date	Hour	Summary of Events and Information	Remarks and references to Appendices
DIVISIONAL RESERVE — NOEUX LES MINES	10/4/16		Commanding Officer arranged Athletic + other Company Competitions as Company Commander has completed the Required Support down in PUIS 14 BIS Section. The day started by O.R. washing on leave between 9.30 + 10 am. The enemy attempted an air raid on the NOEUX-HOUCHIN line. Two A.A. machines were seen to open area of huts. Bombs were dropped in the vicinity of the Sgns at NOEUX LES MINES. Sympathy was shown in proper fashion. The wounded squadron HOUCHIN by men fired from Eq/S. There were no casualties in this Battalion.	
	11/4/16		Advance parties for the Battalion LA NOEUX LES MINES to take over the Report Support line in PUIS 14 BIS Section. The Battalion handed over Bracketh Room at 9.30 p.m. under the Commanding Officer. Arrived the HQ Support Section. Gatting it. Arrived at the Advanced Command at HULLY-HULLUCH. 1st Lt Major. Capt J.R. Sheldrick, Lieuts. M.J. Casey, G.P. Roche, D.J.Bailey 9/5725 Sgt W. Thompson, Lt Col. T Jones, 4/77S, Pt.P. Kelly, 9/4967 Pt. J.O. Sullivan. 9/246 St. Hannaghan J, 9/1912 Lt A Sharpton, Lieut. T.R. Callan were appointed transport Officer. in lieu of Capt... Lt. D.T. Newaghn was appointed Machine Gun officer in lieu Lieut Cutter. 2/Lieut F. Holland reported for duty and was attached to "C" Company	
	12/4/16		The Battalion relieved the 7(S) Bn Royal Innskillen Fusiliers in Report Support line of PUIS 14 BIS Section, proceeded in companies 5th Coy Road at PHILOSOPHE where he was handed thence by Platoons and guides to the positions. The Takeover. The Companies were disposed as follow "A Coy" in 65 METRE POINT REDOUBT + NORTHERN SAP REDOUBT. "B" + "C" Cons in 10th AVENUE. "D" Coy in GUN ALLEY. The relief was completed at 5 pm. The weather was wet throughout. An Cad Stat affair. The Commanding Officer proceeded on leave to England leaving Major V. Kelly in Command of the Battalion Capt Coffin, C2SS. Bollon R.S.F. to Second in Command. A Corps Order.	

Sgd. Morrison
Comdg: 9th (S) Bn. Royal Munster Fusiliers

Army Form C. 2118.

WAR DIARY
or
INTELLIGENCE SUMMARY.
(Erase heading not required.) 9(S) Bn. Royal Munster Fusiliers

Place	Date	Hour	Summary of Events and Information	Remarks and references to Appendices
TRENCHES BDE SUPPORT PLUS 14 BIS SECTION	13/4/16		10th AVENUE FROM 65 METRE POINT REDOUBT TO POSEN ALLEY was cleared. Much additional overhang, all parapets in front of the REDOUBTS. The trench was repaired. Revetted. Shelters were constructed and a garrison. BUSH Johnson was dug where already existing was imperfect. The work on the other REDOUBTS & 9th AVENUE was resumed & found 10th inadequate in every respect. The Battalion always found it necessary working parties of 16 NCOs & 100 men to 250 Tunnellers Coy. R.E. — it had to work in four six hour reliefs each day. Capt Inysell commanding a 3 O.R. McCord & 5 Short leave started until the 1st inst. By 6 o'clock pm all leave was cancelled for 12th inst. the party was recalled at once in the afternoon. It is very necessary to protect our line N.W. of HOHRUCH with first class barbed wire. The Coys Commander under the Command of the Battalion.	
	14/4/16		In 10th AVENUE 8 dugouts were partially reclaimed, the Trench Boards were raised and beneath, the parapets were revetted, the firesteps improved. 9th AVENUE was another trench stopped from a bright post from its junction with POSEN ALLEY, the parapets were repaired and strengthened. In the REDOUBTS 2 Shelters & officers latrines, recesses for S.A.A & bombs. 20' of the Trench were raised of the existing dugouts were cleared. Its line was on the W. from 18 cords of loan were introduced in front of GUN ALLEY. 20' of loan was completed between CHALK PIT ALLEY & POSEN ALLEY. The enemy were observed to shell our line N.W. of HOHRUCH ROAD between 6.17 p.m. They also shelled the VILLAGE LINE S. of 65 METRE POINT REDOUBT intermittently with shrapnel during the day. One shrapnel burst full as a result of heavy artillery fire at 1.48 p.m.	
	15/4/16		In 10th AVENUE further progress was made in improving the trench, cutting firesteps, re-checking dugouts. In 9th AVENUE work on the parapet was continued. A GUN ALLEY & upper 9th Step was emptied 160' of Trench Boards were laid down to 16th m. of CHALK PIT ALLEY & NORTHERN SAP REDOUBT. The parapet of fire step was revetted with sand bags. 12 Coils of wire were introduced into the entanglement F. 65 of 65 METRE POINT REDOUBT A.B. & C. Coy were ordered at 10.9 pm to send their Lewis Gun portion. At 10.20 p.m. a notification was sent to Brigade that this had been done. The Commanding officer and his adjutant 1st Coy Commanders recommend Right	

Army Form C. 2118.

WAR DIARY
or
INTELLIGENCE SUMMARY.

(Erase heading not required.) 9(S) Bn Royal Munster Fusiliers

Instructions regarding War Diaries and Intelligence Summaries are contained in F. S. Regs., Part II. and the Staff Manual respectively. Title pages will be prepared in manuscript.

Place	Date	Hour	Summary of Events and Information	Remarks and references to Appendices
TRENCHES R. SUB-SECTION PUITS 14 BIS SECTION	16/4/16		The Battalion relieved the 7th Bn Royal Irish Rifles in the R. right Subsection of PUITS 14 BIS Section. The Companies were disposed as follows: B Coy. on the right, C coy. in the Centre D coy. on the left. A coy in Reserve. Ration parties from all companies were left at the CRUCIFIX in charge of 2/Lieut. Holland to await the Transport. The relief was completed at 9 pm. The trenches were in a very poor state of repair, & all trenches & communication trenches with the exception of ENGLISH ALLEY shallow and half thrown in were quiet on our front save to some shelling of the town of LOOS during which the armoury town of LOWER BRIDGE was destroyed.	Watchhouse Lt: Colonel Comdg: 9th (S) Bn. Royal Munster Fusiliers
	17/4/16		Work was begun on trenches & Bayonets which were deepened. The parapets were made bullet proof, also shelters and it was substantially built also road traps & obstructing posts on our retrenchment were enhanced. A patrol was sent out to examine the condition of the wire on our front, reported that it was almost non-existant except in a few places where knife rests had been placed to close the gaps. No enemy at all was noticed by the patrol. Also a few working parties were observed at various points on the front, & dispersed by Machine Gun R.M. fire. An enemy Maxim was in action against a suspected look-out post at 7 pm. Immediately afterwards the enemy fell on supports line with 15 M shells. There was some enemy rifle grenades & a trench mortar firing for two/and the night. The 13th Brigade on our Right Spread a hand at 2.50 am, while at 12 midnight the enemy was expected to explode in front of SEAFORTH ALLEY. The Battalion stood to from midnight, when the German mine did not go up, until 4 am. No abnormal activity was caused on our front.	W
	18/4/16		Our Trench was cleared along an entire front. Revetments of the parapet were commenced when the weather necessary. Recesses were deepened & breastplates, 3 Shelters were pulled down and reconstructed times 2 ft x 5 ft bullets were erected. A communication trench to the Bright Bean Store was begun, GORDON ALLEY was deepened. 120 × 5 were erected before the Supports line large Squad under the 2/Lt Casey. The intervening in post from self enemy into strengthened. Enemy snipers were suspected at two points in our front line to the left. Thundering officer & working parties were observed. Myself three shots during the night and dispersed all Machine Gun fire.	W

WAR DIARY or INTELLIGENCE SUMMARY

Army Form C. 2118.

9(S) Bn Royal Munster Fusiliers

Place	Date	Hour	Summary of Events and Information	Remarks and references to Appendices
TRENCHES RIGHT SUB-SECTION PUITS 14 BIS SECTION	19/4/16		Our Support line, ENGLISH ALLEY was shelled & will 18 pm Shell at 8 am 6.2 pm Our Snipers report 2 hits. The Commanding Officer returned from leave.	
	19/4/16		Work in progress on fire steps continued. & the trench board track was again repaired & the trench pits round the cheese over bay. The putties which had been erected on the fire step before were removed & the Reserve C. dispatched. When it had fallen in on 6 dugouts were damaged & destroyed. Wiring on fifty bay was continued. Official reports respecting damage from shell fire. They report that the condition of men in trenches had ceased. Our Snipers claim 3 hits. About 4.15 pm the enemy sent acting will camel cylinder on our Right flank but attacks with all grenades. Our Reserve lives to Battle between 7 & 8 am with 1% shells which did some damage to the trench. Scouts operating continued at a rate as an Rifle Coy front. The adjutant returned from leave.	
	20/4/16		The work on fire trenches continued. GORDON ALLEY & RAILWAY ALLEY were deepened. SCOTS ALLEY & ENGLISH ALLEY were cleaned. 2 living habits build, strengthened to entrenchment in part of our firing line. Patrols were sent out. Lieutenant Desmond, 2 N.C.O.'s & enemy wire (front they noticed a gap in the wire 10' W. of 8/S.4.7 - enquiries are obtained & dispatched upon further Germans W. was actually noticed 9/2/12.6.213. An enemy working party at S.P.7 day. Between 7 & 8 P.M. The enemy bombarded the SUSSEX ROAD, Grenade trench, H.E. shells. Our battalion was relieved with 7/4 Bn Royal Irish Rifles & Battalion Headquarters with Leamy Reserve line at PHILOSOPHE EAST, arriving at 1 am. The men were in excellent spirits. Casualties during tour of trenches from 12.4.16 — 20.4.16: Killed No. 9/5443. Wounded: No. 9/5582, 9/5467, 9/2605, 9/1489, 9/1325.	

M Whitby Barton Lt. Colonel

Comdg: 9th (S) Bn. Royal Munster Fusiliers

Army Form C. 2118.

WAR DIARY
or
INTELLIGENCE SUMMARY.
(Erase heading not required.)

9(S) Bn. Royal Munster Fusiliers

Place	Date	Hour	Summary of Events and Information	Remarks and references to Appendices
PHILOSOPHE EAST	21/4/16		The Battalion in Royal Reserve at PHILOSOPHE EAST. The Billets were daily subjected to the effects of shell fire. Immediate steps were taken to clean lime to dispose of the empty tins & other refuse lying about in the houses & on the roads. The Commanding officer inspected the billets at 11 a.m. During the afternoon Batt. & Regt. Hors. & Cook kitchens were commenced for each Company under the Supervision of Capt. T.M. Belton. A/15 Coys. were marched to baths at MAZINGARBE. The Battalion found various fatigue parties for the R.E & ration parties for the Traffic Manager at VICTORIA STATION. From 7.0.5 – 9.30 p.m. the enemy artillery directed by observation balloons, shelled PHILOSOPHE EAST with 9.2" H.E. Shells. There were no casualties in the Battalion.	
	22/4/16		Work on the Company wash houses & Cook kitchens was continued, other work working parties were found. The roofs of some of the Billets were improved by replacing the tiles. C & D Coys. marched to baths at MAZINGARBE. The day was cloudy & mild.	
	23/4/16		The Battalion parades for Divine Service as follows: R.C. at the Nunnery PHILOSOPHE at 9 am C of E. at 11.2 Field Ambulance at 2 P.M. Work on the Wash houses & Cook kitchens was continued. An incinerator was built. Trifling by the fire was to an 6" guns shelled the enemy lines heavily during the day.	
	24/4/16		The Battalion relieved the 7th Bn Royal Irish Rifles in the Right subsection of PUITS 14 BIS Sect. The Companies were disposed as follows: A Coy on the Right. C Coy on the Centre. D Coy on the Left, B Coy in reserve. The relief was reported complete at 11.15 P.M. The trenches were found to be still in a state of ill repair & required parapets, wire, shelters, fire steps revetting, all the Communication trenches were shallow & dangerous. There was much mud & water everywhere in consequence of the heavy rain	

Army Form C. 2118.

WAR DIARY
or
INTELLIGENCE SUMMARY.

(Erase heading not required.) 9 (S) Bn. Royal Munster Fusiliers

Place	Date	Hour	Summary of Events and Information	Remarks and references to Appendices
TRENCHES RIGHT SUB-SECTION PUITS 14 BIS SECTION	25/4/16		In the trench near the head was cleared so as to undergo a soft manner throughout its length in daylight. Those portions which had fallen in as result of the rain between RAILWAY and ENGLISH ALLEYS were repaired and revetted. Platoon dugouts in small cliff near between RAILWAY and ENGLISH ALLEYS & SCOTS ALLEYS (+100 Y of BOYAU 4) were cleared down as begun in the Support Reserve & English Lines. During the day there were exchanges of Rifle Grenades in which we had the advantage. During the night enemy working parties at several points on his front especially Z.14.Y.1. when he was heard 7.15 am the enemy was active with Small H.E. Shell, & Trench Mortars on our Rifle Grenade, & Riflemen. fires. been tackled by our Trench Mortars, were dispersed by our Machine Gun Rifle fire. Between	
	26/4/16		Work was continued on the parapets & repairs of the trenches & supports. further progress was made on the new dugouts. The Staffs were timbered up to stay high form. 15ft of a new BOYAU to connect front Sup. front time between GORDON & CAMERON ALLEYS was completed, & 30Y of a communicating trench to join GORDON ALLEY the Support BOYAU 7 was repaired. 30Y of wire was erected between H21.4 & H21.5. A patrol from our Centre Coy. reported that no work was in progress in the enemy Sup. "S" on their immediate front, but that the sound of trams, & drums, or trucks, & considerable tooling of the Line, & of the Line, together with much movement in the trenches & ammoned activity on the part of their Snipers. The working party at the Mound S. of PUITS 14 BIS was again detected & dispersed by our Machine Guns. At 3.45 am a heavy Cannonade was heard on our Right in the direction of SOUCHEZ Between & 9.9 pm the enemy Shelled our trenches and Support lines with Shell High Calibre, doing little damage.	

Comdg: 9th (S) Bn. Royal Munster Fus.

Army Form C. 2118.

WAR DIARY
or
INTELLIGENCE SUMMARY.
(Erase heading not required.) 9(S) Bn. Royal Munster Fusiliers

Place	Date	Hour	Summary of Events and Information	Remarks and references to Appendices
TRENCHES RIGHT SUBSECTION PUITS 14 BIS SECTION.	27/4/16		Work proceeded on the Nelson dugouts, trench maintenance. At 5.50 a.m. the enemy fired a salvo from guns & all calibres on the left of our front. As soon as the Shell burst gas was observed drifting very slowly towards our line opposite PUITS 14 BIS. The S.O.S. alarm was given + all units had around them Gas Helmets by 5.57 a.m. The enemy artillery opened vigorously on all parts of the front, putting a barrage of fire on all communication trenches at the same time the enemy intense trench M/G battalion on our left, moving over with the gas. Refining their trenches before it had been shut off. The battalion was not seen from our line. One machine gun on a rifle fire was heard. Two platoons and a party of grenadiers were sent to the assistance of the Battalion on our left. The attack lasted from 10 to 15 minutes. Enemy aeroplanes were observed flying very low over our trenches + to repair or report. They were driven off by our machine guns. A hostile aeroplane flying at 7.15 p.m. attempted to launch 4 gas cylinders at PUITS 14 BIS from which dense clouds of greenish yellow gas were seen to issue. Most seemingly in a Southerly direction. This was thought to be the preliminary of a fire attack on our R/F Coy. The artillery opened on the enemy trench line, destroying many of his works. A patrol under 2/Lt. Murphy reported two posts of the enemy were sufficiently strong below a Small party to approach our front & Small light volleys was located in the front. Along which working material was brought to a point in front of our left company. The enemy were reported to be carrying gas cylinders were observed near PUITS 14 BIS. The enemy also reported to be moving at various points. Their front when they were fired on by our artillery, Rifles + Machine Guns.	M
	28/4/16		All work visited by tow men from 11th Hants. Enemy repaired the portion of our line which had been disturbed by the bombardment of the preceding day. E.W. Ryan Lt Col Comdg: 9th (S) Bn. Royal Munster F	M

Army Form C. 2118.

WAR DIARY
or
INTELLIGENCE SUMMARY.
(Erase heading not required.)

9 (S) Bn. Royal Munster Fusiliers

Instructions regarding War Diaries and Intelligence Summaries are contained in F.S. Regs., Part II and the Staff Manual respectively. Title pages will be prepared in manuscript.

Place	Date	Hour	Summary of Events and Information	Remarks and references to Appendices
TRENCHES RIGHT SUB-SECTION PUITS 14 BIS SECTION	28/4/16		About 5.30 a.m. the enemy opened a heavy bombardment upon Right company & in the trenches that suffered most were GORDON ALLEY, CAMERON ALLEY, the junction of the latter with SCOTS ALLEY. The shell that caused the greatest damage came from the direction of HULLUCH & may have been fired from the train that was distinctly heard there during the night. The bombardment was directed from Balloon aeroplane. A number of Many Minen wer also sent up by the enemy to assist their artillery. Our trench mortar machine guns were in action against their Minen & several points without effect. A reply to it call of our Right Company, our artillery opened against the enemy had, in their full burst to high side the left. Gas clouds were also observed towards between 6 + 7 a.m. near PUITS 14 BIS. They were believed to contain effects lights and contain the usual poison (no. At 3 p.m. an machine gun was driven away by the aircraft that were firing lots over our lines. At 9.30 p.m. an artillery in answer to a false report of gas bile N. of HULLUCH bombarded the enemies line vigorously for 40 minutes. There was no retaliation. A reinforcing draft of 24 OR arrived for the Battalion.	
	29/4/16		The trenches were cleaned and repaired when they showed the effects of yesterdays bombardment. At 8.30 a.m. the enemy sent up according to a report 8 white rockets or red rockets, ceasing to another, 2 green rockets and 1 a gun. Immediately afterwards a jet of greenish yellow gas was observed from the PUITS 14 BIS stand at a rate that did not exceed 1 1/2 miles an hour towards the left subsection. The wind carried the fumes clean over LA Coy front the changing later into an unknown trench which they could afford to go yards, all ranks had movement then helmets, stage were hung against it. gas, hand which only on casualty was suffered. Shortly afterwards the wind again changed carries the gas away Otto' small. The attack was supported by a fight bombardment.	

Comdg: 9th (S) Bn. Royal Munster Fusiliers

Army Form C. 2118.

WAR DIARY
or
INTELLIGENCE SUMMARY.

(Erase heading not required.)

9 (S) Bn. Royal Munster Fusiliers

Instructions regarding War Diaries and Intelligence Summaries are contained in F. S. Regs., Part II. and the Staff Manual respectively. Title pages will be prepared in manuscript.

Place	Date	Hour	Summary of Events and Information	Remarks and references to Appendices
TRENCHES RIGHT SUBSECTION PUITS 1A BIS SECTION	29/4/16		Our artillery replying sent several shells into the enemy trenches. Our machine guns also fired fire when it was observed that enemy endeavoured to leave their line on our front. Our artillery machine guns were instructed to sweep his parapet in front of their subsection. Enemy aeroplanes were very active above our trenches, when they were engaged by our machine guns. During the morning the enemy shot down one of our aeroplanes in the direction of PHILOSOPHE. At 11.15 am an enemy aeroplane was seen to fall behind our line at VERMELLES. The Battalion was relieved by the 6th Bn. Royal Irish Regiment (proceeded to Divisional Rest Huts) at MAZINGARBE. The relief was completed at 11.50 pm. The Spirit of the men was excellent. Casualties during tour of the Trenches 24/4/16 - 29/4/16. Killed: 2/Lt P.T. O'Flynn & 7 O.R. Wounded: 28 O.R. Missing: 6 O.R.	W/ W/
MAZINGARBE	30/4/16		The Battalion were employed in cleaning huts etc. Inspections of arms equipment to clean defensible were held by all companies. The Major at Retreat	W/

F. W. Cartwright Bond
Lt: Col:
Comdg: 9th (S) Bn. Royal Munster Fusiliers

May 1916

Army Form C. 2118.

WAR DIARY
or
INTELLIGENCE SUMMARY.
(Erase heading not required.)

Vol 5
XVI
9 Bn Royal Munster Fusiliers

Place	Date	Hour	Summary of Events and Information	Remarks and references to Appendices
MAZING-ARBE	1/5/16		The Battalion found various fatigues and carrying parties for the I Corps Signallers, the R.E. & also a burying party from the 8 Dublins under 2/Lt Holland. Major H.J. Williams late officer Commanding the Battalion died in England. 2/Lt Carey took over command of "D" coy during the absence of Capt. Weigel (on leave). The Band played at Retreat at 6.30 p.m.	
	2/5/16		fatigue & carrying parties as above. All Companies paraded for Battn at MAZINGARBE. 2/Lt Hartnett was appointed French Master (Officer i/c 2/Lt O'Flynn (killed in action) and proceeded to ST. VENANT to indulge a course of instruction. Capt Harding and 4 O.R. proceeded on leave. There was a lecture in Cinema Theatre NOEUX LES MINES on Mine Warfare for officers & senior non commissioned officers.	
	3/5/16		fatigues & carrying parties for the I Corps, & R.E. Information was received that the Army Commander would inspect the Battalion at NOEUX LES MINES on the succeeding day. The Battalion paraded at the huts at 6.30 p.m. when it was inspected by Brigadier General Pennsary D.S.O., & the commanding officer presented to Pte. 9/1729 Baly T., & 9/4575 Sealy T. the Divisional Parchment Certificate for conspicuous courage displayed on April 27th 1916 in bringing in wounded under fire.	
	4/5/16		fatigues & carrying parties as above. Such of the men as were not on fatigue were exercised in the rapid adjustment of gas helmets. The enemy shelled MAZINGARBE in the vicinity of the Huts. There were no casualties. The inspection arrived for this day was cancelled. Instead a selected platoon from the Battalion was ordered to parade with platoons from the other Battalions in the Brigade at NOEUX LES MINES on the 5th inst. for inspection by the Corps Commander.	
	5/5/16		fatigues & carrying parties as above. One platoon of "D" coy under 2/Lt Gleeson was inspected with the Commanding officer in appreciation of the splendid manner at NOEUX LES MINES. It marched through the conduct of all ranks in the Trenches. 48th Brigade Horse Show at NOEUX LES MINES.	

F.W.S. Stephenson Lt. Colonel,
Comdg: 9th (S) Bn. Royal Munster Fusiliers.

WAR DIARY or INTELLIGENCE SUMMARY

Army Form C. 2118.

9 Bn Royal Munster Fusiliers

Place	Date	Hour	Summary of Events and Information	Remarks and references to Appendices
MAZING- ARBE	5/5/16		Out of 9 events the Battalion obtained the highest total of distinctions, with 4 first places, 3 second, 1 third, including the first 3 second places for Officers' Charges, which were won by the Commanding Officer (Capt. Stack Dick, Capt. Oletelu) 4a O.R. proceeded on leave.	
TRENCHES LEFT SUB- SECTION HULLUCH SECTION	6/5/16		The Battalion relieved the 9th Bn Royal Irish Fusiliers in the Left Subsection of the HULLUCH Section, proceeding by platoons at 100 yds interval via PHILOSOPHE (VERMELLES) to the trenches. The relief was reported complete at 4.0 p.m. The Battalion was disposed as follows: C Coy on the Right, A Coy in trenches, B Coy on the Left, in Reserve D Coy. 2nd Lt. Baily was appointed "O.C. Craters". Capt. D.M. Batson, previously in charge of the front line, & Lt. Quigan, returning from hospital, took over the Transport from Lt. Cobbe, who returned to the Machine Gun Section.	
	7/5/16		The trenches had been handed over in a bad state of repair. Steam wall salvage on Sunday. Work was begun in all companies to remedy this. Strong squads from C, A & B Coys. overhauled & added its sort work to already existing in our front. There were some exchanges of rifle grenades throughout the day. What appeared to be a Young Gun party between the craters ran a sap in the enemy line, which them towards the mine cavity on our Right Coy front. Our Stokes Mortars played with fresh accuracy on the enemy on the proposed artillery retaliation.	
	8/5/16		The work of cleaning the line of salvage, repairs was continued when the trenches had been blown in by shellfire they were put in a proper state of defence by first night. Throughout examination of the parapets, a strong mining party under Lt. Casey together with a working squad from the 7 Bn. Royal Irish Rifles set out to construct a system of attachments between the craters of the three fields on our centre Coy. front. Officers' patrols sent out from all companies to examine the condition of the enemies wire reported that except on our Left Coy. front which had been severely damaged by our mines trench mortars, it was very formidable. No saps had been cut in recently. No New a small mine at 3 a.m. between MUNSTER & TRALEE CRATERS. Our Artillery, Grenadiers, Machine Guns opened fire. The situation was again normal before 5 am. No new crater was formed. An hostile aeroplane having circled our lines was observed on its return to drop a cluster of white lights. Nothing unusual resulted.	

F. Whitaker Brodie Lt. Colonel
Comdg. 9th (S) Bn Royal Munster Fusiliers

Army Form C. 2118.

WAR DIARY or INTELLIGENCE SUMMARY.

(Erase heading not required.) 9 Bn. Royal Munster Fusiliers

Place	Date	Hour	Summary of Events and Information	Remarks and references to Appendices
TRENCHES LEFT SUB-SECTION HULLUCH SECTION	9/5/16		Work on the defences of the front line Sap line was continued. STRAW ALLEY was pre-stopped for 18' with a view to flank defence. The dugouts in the Right company were cleaned, revised, habitable. Oilsplints proofs reinforced with layers of sandbags. The Special mining party in charge of Lt. Casey continued to work under the supervision of the Commanding Officer. An enemy Trench Mortar bombarded the enemy's line effectively attaining 3 direct hits on a small work at H.13.a.3.6. An enemy Machine Gun, which swept our parapets entirely, but an enemy mining party was located in a small crater. Men by the Divisional MUNSTER & TRALEE CRATERS. On discovery it was had its base of by our Trench Mortars. Various small working parties observed in the enemy's line were dispersed with rifle grenades. Sounds of enemy mining were reported by the R.E. at No 7 Sap also by a listening party in our Left Coy front. The Tunnelling Officer was informed. He failed to detect them. Towards noon all coys were relieved	
	10/5/16		Work on the defences of the front line Sap line continued. FIV LANE reopened for a length of 17'. The trenches was cleaned & revetted where they had fallen in owing to rain. Two small mines were sprung by the enemy – Lip of TRALEE CRATER, the smaller on the Northern lip of SMITHS CRATER. Our Machine Guns opened fire on the approaches to the craters. None of the bombers who had been fatally entombed by the former explosion were retrieved. The commanding officer & a party reconnoitred TRALEE CRATER shortly afterwards. Surprise fire of the enemy on the Parapets. One was killed by our Guns. At 1 a.m. an Irishman surprised 5 of the enemy at the bottom of TRALEE CRATER. 3 were killed. The Special Mining Party in charge of Lt. Casey continued its work on the mine pits under the personal supervision of the Commanding Officer. They were harassed by enemy Machine Gun fire & Lt. Casey was slightly wounded. An artillery duel & enemy working party in this position obtaining 3 direct hits. Details from all coys in turn dug in, to admit of no enemy working parties had been a contact this line. We incurred 54/= in our wire. The Battalion was relieved by the 7 Bn. Royal Irish Rifles. Proceeded to Life Support Battalion area in 10th AVENUE, with exception of D coy sent with it to RESERVE TRENCH.	
	11/6/16		The Battalion found the following fatigues: 1 officer & 40 OR in fair order for the 253 Tunnelling Coy R.E. 42 OR for 161/1 A's/R Trench Mortar Batteries (1 Special mining party of 30 OR was sent to work with enemy under 2nd Lt. Green (in the Coy.))	

F. M. Ziegler Brose Lt. Colonel,
Comdg. 9th (S) Bn. Royal Munster Fusiliers

Army Form C. 2118.

WAR DIARY
or
INTELLIGENCE SUMMARY.
(Erase heading not required.)

Instructions regarding War Diaries and Intelligence Summaries are contained in F.S. Regs., Part II. and the Staff Manual respectively. Title pages will be prepared in manuscript.

9 Bn Royal Munster Fusiliers

Place	Date	Hour	Summary of Events and Information	Remarks and references to Appendices
TRENCHES LEFT SUB SECTION HULLUCH SECTION	11/5/16		Of the ah intense bombardment of all calibres which extended to the communication trenches of our subsection & to VERMELLES, MAZINGARBE, & PHILOSOPHE, & lasting from 3.45 to 7 P.H., the enemy penetrated the line of the 15th Divsn. on our left, carrying 500 yds of their front trench. A heavy counter attack supported by bombers + Irishmen Trench Mortar fire at midnight failed to dislodge him.	Nil
	12/5/16		The Battalion found fatigues as on the 11th inst. The Special wiring party continued work on the craters under 2 Lt. Gleeson. General repair of 16th AVENUE was carried on. WINGS WAY was cleared from 10th AVENUE to SUPPORT LINE. There was an intermittent shelling of the communicating trenches N of the HULLUCH ROAD	Nil
	13/5/16		The usual fatigues were found. WINGS WAY & HAY ALLEY were deepened & cleaned. 4th & 9th AVENUE trench traps were constructed. The Battalion relieved the 7 Battalion Royal Irish Rifles in the LEFT SUBSECTION, HULLUCH SECTION. The relief was reported complete at 5.55 p.m. The Battalion was disposed as follows. A Coy. in RESERVE; B Coy. on the Left; D Coy. in the Centre; C Coy. on the Right.	Nil
	14/5/16		The Battalion was employed clearing the trenches of mud & rewetting the parapets where they had fallen in in consequence of the bad weather. Fatigue parties were found for R.R.E. & Trench Mortar Batteries. A special wiring party worked in the Mine field under intermittent Machine Gun fire. Patrols from all companies in the front line went out to report on the condition of the enemy wire. A violent artillery duel took place on our left in the direction of the KINK in which the enemy appeared to have the advantage in weight of projectiles.	Nil

F. Montagu Bradd
Lt. Colonel
9th Bn (S) Royal Munster Fusiliers

WAR DIARY
or
INTELLIGENCE SUMMARY.

(Erase heading not required.)

Army Form C. 2118.

1 Bn. Royal Munster Fusiliers

Place	Date	Hour	Summary of Events and Information	Remarks and references to Appendices
TRENCHES LEFT SUB-SECTION HULLUCH SECTION	15.5.16		Repair of Trenches continued. At 4.30 p.m. all Companies in the Front line in conjunction with the Redoubt supply Trench Mortar Batteries bombarded the enemy line with Rifle Grenades for 15 minutes. Sounds of enemy running were suspected at several points in our front line, reported to the Commanding Officer.	
	16.5.16		Work on Trenches continued. The Front line which the Battalion took over was designed for 5B. The Battalion was relieved by the 15th Division & proceeded to the Brigade Support Line in the RIGHT SUBSECTION, PUITS 14 BIS SECTION, which it took over from the 8th Bn. Royal Irish Regiment. The Companies were disposed as follows: in GUN ALLEY B Coy: in NORTHERN SAP & 65 METRE POINT REDOUBTS, A Coy; in 1st AVENUE, D Coy; 1C Coy less 2 Platoons. The remaining 2 Platoons of C Coy. proceeded to PHILOSOPHE under the Command of 2nd Lieut D.J. O'Callaghan to provide pushing parties for the Brigade. Lt. N.F. Casey proceeded on leave to Ireland with 3 O.R.	
	17.5.16		Clearing & improvement of the Trenches commenced by all Companies. New dugouts & latrines were put under construction in GUN ALLEY. Wiring parties worked on the entanglement w. of 65 METRE POINT REDOUBT. Fatigue & carrying parties were found for the R.E. at the Trench Mortar Batteries. A violent bombardment was observed in the direction of the KINK from 6.30 - 6 p.m. in the course of which small shells appeared to be used.	
	18.5.16		Work on the Trenches & Redoubts continued. Fatigue parties were found as above. Between 1.30 & 2.30 p.m. the enemy shelled the VILLAGE LINE 100 S. of 65 METRE POINT REDOUBT. Lieut. Usill & 4 O.R. proceeded on leave.	

Fitzgerald Brooke
Lt. Colonel,
1 Bn. Royal Munster Fusiliers

Army Form C. 2118.

WAR DIARY
or
INTELLIGENCE SUMMARY.
(Erase heading not required.)

9th Bn. Royal Munster Fusiliers

Instructions regarding War Diaries and Intelligence Summaries are contained in F. S. Regs., Part II. and the Staff Manual respectively. Title pages will be prepared in manuscript.

Place	Date	Hour	Summary of Events and Information	Remarks and references to Appendices
TRENCHES RIGHT SUB-SECTION. PUITS 14 BIS SECTION	19.5.16		Work on Trenches was continued + fatigue parties found as above. From about 3.30 – 4.30 p.m. the enemy shelled FOSSE 7 & QUALITY STREET with heavy H.E. Shell. Emplacements for a bath & water cart were constructed in 10th AVENUE.	MW
PUITS 14 BIS SECTION	20.5.16		The Battalion relieved the 7th Bn. Royal Irish Rifles in the front line of the RIGHT SUBSECTION PUITS 14 BIS SECTION. The relief was reported complete at 6.20 p.m. The Battalion was disposed as follows reading from left to right, all 4 Companies being in the front line. "A" Coy, "C" Coy, "B" Coy, "D" Coy. Patrols were sent out by all Companies & working parties front & support tools were repaired wherever they had suffered from shell fire. Platoon dugouts were started in each company front.	MW
	21.5.16		Work on Trench Maintenance & Platoon dugouts was continued. Patrols during halts were sent out & was composed of a patrol from "C" Coy under command of Capt. Fletcher brought in a Notice that had been observed in front of the enemy wire on the preceding day. "A read" Request for cleaner explication by written or personally." (sic) At 11.50 p.m. we opened a bombardment of the enemy front line & particularly PUITS 14 BIS with Rifle Grenades, Trench Mortar Guns, Stokes Guns, Machine Guns in conjunction with the Artillery. Working parties on his wire & in his front line trench were subjected to this which continued until shortly after 250 bombs. Their retaliation was late & ineffective. We repeated the bombardment at 1.10 a.m.	MW
	22.5.16		Work on Trench Maintenance & Platoon dugouts was continued. Patrols & working parties were sent out by all companies. One of the former received from the enemy trench a bullet board which had evidently been torn by them from our Wire the Battalion took over Sub-section. It was after the Notice that the "Extrication of yesterday referred. An effort entitled "SIR ROGER CASEMENT" was had been supposed in trench from a new Wiring Wire patrols yesterday was brought in. It appeared to annoy the enemy who found the middle will letters.	MW

F. Montagu Brooke, Lt: Colonel,
Comdg. 9th (S) Bn. Royal Munster Fusiliers.

Army Form C. 2118.

WAR DIARY
or
INTELLIGENCE SUMMARY. 9th Royal Munst. Fusiliers

(Erase heading not required.)

Place	Date	Hour	Summary of Events and Information	Remarks and references to Appendices
TRENCHES RIGHT SUB-SECTION PUITS 14 BIS SECTION.	23/5/16		Work on Trench Maintenance & Wiring dugouts was continued. Wiring parties were sent out by all Companies. At 1 P.M. an Battalion Company Bombers crawled out to the enemy entanglement & bombed them towards. At places where patties were near the enemy. Judging by the groans heard considerable casualties must have been caused. 6 Machine Guns which had been fired from a point 200 x S of PUITS 14 BIS was also effectually bombed. All our bombers returned without casualty. At 2.25 P.M. the enemy showing that we had irritated him, put up a heavy barrage along the fire trench in the direction of PUITS 14 BIS.	
	24/5/16		Work on Trench Maintenance & Platoon Dug outs was continued. Wiring parties were sent out by all companies. Between 12.45 P.M. bombing parties from "A" & "B" Coys crawled out though the enemy entanglement when it had been reached by our bombing T.M. and 2 grenades. showered the trench & obs. grenades. The party from A. Coy. located one of 2 Machine guns. with heavy S.A.A. at H2d. 5.6. & sealed a working party near them with rifle fire. The enemy line was entered by 2 L.S.P. and three German his at close range. While on their way back to C. Coy Trench a wiring party met Lt. LENS-LA BASSÉE ROAD, who fired in chords leaving 6 officers wounded in the ground. The party from B Coy. located 2.5" with enemy S.A.A. Trench in the vicinity of SPS 5 + 6. There were two Maxim Gun detached. also & enfiladed but not been actioned. On repeated use 2 L.L. Shrub, slightly wounded. a 2 cm. wounded. The enemy opened an artillery also with trench mortars also 250 bomb in it were taken by the wiring parties. The Gnoom & C.S.M. Typer learnt them from after dry break & issued for all the early found him safely would reach the enemy wire. Comrades him safely & their lives under heavy Machine Gun fire.	

M. Leigh Brodie
Lt. Colonel.
Comdg; 9th (S) Bn. Royal Munster Fusiliers.

Army Form C. 2118.

WAR DIARY
or
INTELLIGENCE SUMMARY. 9th Royal Munster Fusiliers

(Erase heading not required.)

Instructions regarding War Diaries and Intelligence Summaries are contained in F. S. Regs., Part II. and the Staff Manual respectively. Title pages will be prepared in manuscript.

Place	Date	Hour	Summary of Events and Information	Remarks and references to Appendices
TRENCHES RIGHT SUB SECTION PUITS 14 BIS SECTION	25.5.16		Work on Trench Maintenance & Platoon Dug outs was continued. Patrols covering parties were sent out by all Companies. An enemy raiding Party of 16 men with 2 machine guns was surprised by our patrol consisting of 3 men before it could reach our wire. On exchange of bomb throwing in which one of the Patrol was wounded under cover of which the enemy withdrew. Shortly afterwards Searchlight was directed on the Patrol & among the group with which Platoon Pumps of the enemy 3r Spl Sgt (Tactical Leader Sergt Shea assisted by Pt Shea Nichy Pt Patal succeeded in regaining the wounded man & conveying him in safety from the The Battalion was relieved by the 6th Bn Royal Irish Regiment (proceeded to rest to the huts at MAZINGARBE. Casualties during Tour of trenches 6.5.16 – 25.5.16: Killed 5 O.R. Officers 2 Lt. M.J. Sheehan, 58 O.R. wounded (at duty) Lt Carey & 2 O.R. Wounded 2 Lt. E. O'Ball. W.	W.
MAZING-ARBE.	26.5.16		In view of the afore-mentioned break up of the Battalion by order of the I Corps to provide reinforcements for the 1st & 2nd Battalions, the Commanding Officer invited all officers to a farewell dinner at MAZINGARBE	W.
	27.5.16		Acting on orders from the 48th INF. BDE. the Battalion was held in readiness to move at half an hours notice.	W.
DROUVIN.	28.5.16		The Battalion leaving the 48th INF. BDE. Area, in which they were replaced by the 19th Battalion R.W.F., proceeded to Billets at DROUVIN. The leaving of the men was excellent, they were compatible with Division Ground then marched past other NOEUX LES MINES.	W.

E Montagh Brown
Lt. Colonel,
Comdg. 9th (S) Bn. Royal Munster Fusiliers.

Army Form C. 2118.

WAR DIARY
or
INTELLIGENCE SUMMARY.

9th Royal Munster Fusiliers

(Erase heading not required.)

Place	Date	Hour	Summary of Events and Information	Remarks and references to Appendices
DROUVIN	29/5/16		The Battalion paraded for Divine Service in the Church at DROUVIN. Mass was celebrated by the Chaplain & Rev. Fr. Gallen, for the officer NCOs & other Ranks of the Battalion who had fallen in the war.	M
	30/5/16		The Battalion was broken up to form the following reinforcing drafts which left DROUVIN to join their units. for 1st Batⁿ R.M.F.: 6 officers & 253 O.R: for the 2nd Battalion R.M.F: 7 officers & 140 O.R :- for the 8th Battalion R.M.F: 12 officers & 200 O.R. Lieut Colonel E Montagu-Browne took over command of the 8th Battalion at PHILOSOPHE W. In Sir Douglas Haig's Despatches published at this date, the Battalion was mentioned first in the 2nd Division as having been "Specially brought to his notice for good work in carrying out or repelling local attacks & raids."	M

E Montagu-Browne
Lt. Colonel,
Comdg. 9th (S) Bn. Royal Munster Fusiliers.

www.ingramcontent.com/pod-product-compliance
Lightning Source LLC
Chambersburg PA
CBHW081452160426
43193CB00013B/2450